BE BLESSED
Reflections of Introspect

DR. CRYSHAUNDA RORIE

Be Blessed: Reflections of Introspect

Copyright 2021 by Dr. Cryshaunda Rorie.

All rights reserved.

No part of this publication may be reproduced, stored in a retrieval system, or transmitted in any way, by any means whether electronically, mechanically, via photocopy, recording, or otherwise without the prior written permission of the publisher except as provided by USA copyright law.

Published by TJS Publishing House
www.tjspublishinghouse.com
contact@tjspublishinghouse.com

Cover design by FF Designs

Published in the United States of America.
ISBN-13: 978-1-952833-27-4
ISBN-10: 1-952833-27-2

DEDICATION

I dedicate this work to myself. Shaunda, I am so proud of you. Your courage, your motivation, your strength is unmatched. You haven't always been here, but damn, doesn't it feel good! Keep being the best version of yourself while growing through whatever life has for you. Your love, your light and your passion need to be heard, seen & felt. Thank you for never giving up, and girl…

Be Blessed.

Heyyyyy! So, I'm Cryshaunda, but by now, you probably already know that. Either you are a friend, colleague, family member, hater, and fan or simply walked past this book cover and said, "Yes! She looks like she has something to say!" No matter how you found this masterpiece, I'm glad you did!

I pray my reflection of introspecting spark your thoughts, challenge your soul and help you become a better you. And if none of that happens, honey, "Be Blessed!" So, let's get this reading party started. Grab your snacks, and don't forget your reading glasses because it's about to go down.

CONTENTS

	Acknowledgments	i
1	You Are Not Responsible for How You Grow Up, but You Are Responsible for How You Grow!	1
2	Build Your Foundation and Choose Your Own Contents	15
3	Happiness Is a Choice	21
4	A Stranger Will Support You Before Anyone Else and You Better Not Cry About It!	31
5	Give Yourself Permission to Do What's Right For You	38
6	Make a Difference in the World by Simply Living in It	45
7	Leave Him Where You Met Him; Sometimes	47
8	You're Enough	55
9	Only Consume What Nourishes	61
10	The Devil Doesn't Care	67
11	Unapologetically Dope	73
12	Your Mouth Is Your Weakness, Sis	77
13	Everything You Need Is in You	83
14	Get Out of Your Own Way	91
15	End of Story	97

ACKNOWLEDGMENTS

To:
Geovanni Hood for being my "safe place" & to my mom, Angela Rorie, brother Taquawn Rorie & Legacy Blair Noelle
for being my motivation & unwavering support.
Special thanks to my photographer, Alphonso Abbott (jrsactionshots.com), and to TJS Publishing House for helping me deliver my third book baby!

1

YOU ARE NOT RESPONSIBLE FOR HOW YOU GROW UP, BUT YOU ARE RESPONSIBLE FOR HOW YOU GROW!

BE BLESSED: *REFLECTIONS OF INTROSPECT*

Yeah, I said it, and I went as far as putting it in a book, so you know I mean it. As an adult, accountability will take us far. Blaming your entire life circumstances on mama, daddy, grandma and everything in between does nothing but hinder your growth, make room for negativity and exude "dependent" energy. Learn how to take responsibility for your growth and stop being a sucker for cycles of the unnecessary.

You're probably reading this like, "Danggggg, she came out swinging". Yes, yes, I did. Now carry on! Sometimes we give and give of ourselves for others: managers, clients, parents, spouses, kids, friends, family, neighbors. Whether it's out of love or necessity, a significant part of our day is given over.

We do all these on someone else's terms: their needs, their goals, their dreams. And it isn't necessarily all bad. We have to earn a paycheck and build relationships, which are formed and maintained by exchanging favors and sharing experiences.

Here's the challenge, though. Without the right rhythms for ourselves, we can quickly lose focus of our dreams and what we want from this life. We can quickly lose sight of our needs and our growth.

By spending our days doing things that we believe will make other people happy, we never find time to chase what makes us happy. We never find time to grow and develop our terms.

Plus, it's incredibly difficult to know what will make another person happy. And I'm not saying you shouldn't ever try; I am saying you should make your growth and happiness a priority.

So, I challenge you to take 15 minutes to plan a personal day.

If you had a day to yourself to focus on your growth, what would it look like? Who would you talk to? What would you do?

Design the day. Then reserve a day on your calendar—next week, next month, next year. I recommend four guidelines in the design of your day:

BE BLESSED: *REFLECTIONS OF INTROSPECT*

1. One part of your day, early in the day preferably, should include time with a close friend talking about personal growth and development.
2. Another part has to be independent, on your own. Perhaps a couple of hours of solitude. Make this later in the day, so you have time to reflect on earlier discussions and studies from the day.
3. Keep it simple. Don't try to do too much. Limit your day to four or five activities.
4. Lastly, treat yourself well. Eat well, go for a hike, and stay healthy the entire day. This isn't a day to let yourself go; rather, it's to put your top priorities back into focus.

"One can choose to go back toward safety or forward toward growth. Growth must be chosen again and again; fear must be overcome again and again."

— Abraham Maslow

THERE'S A DIFFERENCE BETWEEN AN AFFIRMATION AND A CONFIRMATION

BE BLESSED: *REFLECTIONS OF INTROSPECT*

af firm a tion
/ˌafərˈmāSH(ə)n/
the action or process of affirming something or being affirmed.
con fir ma tion
/ˌkänfərˈmāSH(ə)n/
the action of confirming something or the state of being confirmed.

So now that we are on the same page, let's dive into this. I see so many millennials affirming things in life. No biggie! Just remember that an affirmation is not confirmation. We can affirm all we want to, but we cannot act on those affirmations until we have received confirmation from our actions. Are you affirming without action? How does that work? Are you affirming without proper planning? Are you affirming without getting organized? Are you affirming without researching? Let's talk about it.

Before confirmation, we use our affirmations to set the tone, create the vibe and prepare us for what's ahead. Confirmation is something that supports, validates, or verifies something else, while affirmation is a positive statement or declaration of the truth or existence of something. So, let's make our own affirmations right now at this moment. I'll start:

- I am in charge of my own happiness. ...
- I accept 100% responsibility for my own life. ...
- The best is yet to come. ..

BE BLESSED: *REFLECTIONS OF INTROSPECT*

Now it's your turn!

_____

_____

_____

_____

_____

Now how do you plan to make these affirmations and confirmations? You have written them, spoken them out loud, and now you have to put faith and action behind them to bring them to fruition. Knowing the difference between an affirmation and a confirmation will get you closer to your goals and beyond. Take a few minutes to think about the plan you will utilize and make a promise to yourself that you will not allow anything or anyone to get in the way of it.

2

BUILD YOUR FOUNDATION AND CHOOSE YOUR OWN CONTENTS

BE BLESSED: *REFLECTIONS OF INTROSPECT*

Never let someone feel like they have the power to build you. You are the architect of your life, so get to building! This retrospect, in a sense, gives us permission to take control, but who asked for it? But I put it in here for a reason. What's the reason? Well, I'm glad you asked!

I am so tired of watching people let others build them up just to tear them down. Yes, your best friend helped you get to a certain point in life but tore you down as soon as the friendship was over because she felt entitled to your becoming. It just happened to you, didn't it? I know, but let's carry on.

The issue here is that we as a people tend to look for confirmation from our peers to build. But let's not forget what we just spoke about a few lines up in this book. Confirmation comes from the actions WE put behind our affirmations, not from what our boos, parents, siblings or co-workers put into action. Take accountability for your foundation. Before we can become equipped with the contents of life, we have to build our foundation strong from the inside out.

BE BLESSED: *REFLECTIONS OF INTROSPECT*

Have you ever thought about whether you have a strong inner foundation that helps to guide your life choices? I mean the inner structure that helps you live your life with less stress and overwhelm?

If your foundation isn't solid, you might feel like life is constantly knocking you down just when things seem to be getting back on track. Even if you already have a sturdy inner foundation, that doesn't mean it can't sway from side to side sometimes. The pressures of the world constantly test our strength, and it can take a lot of effort to stay upright. With a strong inner foundation, you'll be better able to handle the winds of change. You can grow more when you're in a secure space and rooted in what you need and want.

Here are some things to think about when it comes to your own foundation in life:

Mindset

- What thoughts do you need to believe about yourself to feel supported?

- How can you be more mindful of your own feelings and behaviors?

- How can you focus on the current moment more than the past/future?

Values

- What do you value in friendships and relationships? (e.g. a sense of humor, empathy, willingness to challenge you when necessary)

- What do you value in your work? (e.g. flexibility, reliable co-workers, independence)

- What are the top 3 values you want to uphold in your own life? (think about how you want others to describe you)

Habits

- What are your current daily habits?

- Are your habits self-supporting or self-defeating?

- What habits would help make your life feel more balanced?

-

Strengths

- What are your biggest strengths?

- How do these strengths help support you in life?

- How can you make better use of your strengths in your daily life?

Relationships

- What makes you feel most supported in a relationship or friendship?

- Who are the people in your life who make you feel grounded?

- Are there any relationships you need to let go of to feel more stable?

Ultimately, a strong inner foundation is what keeps you balanced, stable, and secure. Come back to this retrospect whenever you notice yourself feeling unsteady. You got it!

3
HAPPINESS IS A CHOICE

BE BLESSED: *REFLECTIONS OF INTROSPECT*

I mean, duh! If I could insert an emoji right here, I would. Definitely the one with the eyes looking up to the ceiling because I mean, who doesn't have time for happiness? Apparently, a lot of people, so that's why it's in this good read of a book.

Now this one may get a little long-winded because I have a lot to say, but you didn't spend your money on just anything, so please don't complain. Happiness is a choice and not a result of achievements or purchases, in my educated opinion. But maintaining your happy vibe isn't always easy. How do I know this? Because I struggle with it all the time. I'm human, too, right?

As many accomplishments I've achieved, you'd be forgiven for thinking that I leap out of bed each morning after a restful sleep with a grin on my face, full of great intentions for the day ahead. Not so! Indeed, for the main part, for me, happiness is a choice rather than my natural state of being.

In fact, like all of us, I'm not happy all the time (let's face it, that would just be *weird*). In reality, for me, authentic happiness doesn't signify a lack of negative feelings such as sadness and pain, but an ability to experience a wide spectrum of emotions while managing to appreciate – and stay focused on – the positive things that I *do* have in my life.

As adults, we have to make a choice to be happy, even when our life circumstances and situations tell us otherwise. And we have to do that over and over and over again.

Choosing to be happy is a constant effort, and to be honest, it's not something that comes naturally. In fact, I've had to train myself to think happy. Indeed, like millions of us, I've struggled with periods of depression and anxiety, had to live with periods of debilitating panic attacks or episodes of rumination that have beaten my mental health and happiness down.

Along the way, I've learned that these problems should not define me or my mood. Indeed, I can still see happiness as a choice, but it requires focus and effort to stay positive.

Happiness fuels success, not vice versa

Most people go through life thinking that happiness is something that happens to them as a result of success or something good happening, for example, getting a pay rise or getting 100 new likes on their latest Instagram post. Indeed, large parts of the population don't realize that happiness is a choice and instead go through the motions in life, waiting for joy to pop up and slap them in the face!

However, science shows that this type of instant gratification doesn't really make us happy (not in the long term, anyway). In fact, there is no magic pill to finding happiness. However, there is one thing that *is* required to boost well-being, and that is work. Work? Ugh! I'm afraid so. Because happiness is a choice, it needs to be worked at consistently, with effort, care and dedication on your behalf.

In fact, I believe the root of happiness is in the work you put into it. You have to commit to being happy, prioritize it, focus on it, and remain disciplined as much as possible, even in those dark and difficult days – *especially* in those dark days!

If happiness is a choice, how can I work on it?

It sounds staggering, but it's reported that we make around 35,000 remotely conscious decisions every single day. From seemingly inconsequential stuff about choosing what to eat and what clothes to wear to bigger things like who to love, how to spend our free time, whether to move to a new city or quit the job we feel stuck in.

Some of our choices turn out to be great, and others not so. What they have in common, though, is that all of these choices are based on our deep desire to be happy.

Okay, I hear what you might be thinking: all of this is easier said than done. Life is tough. Shit happens. Stuff gets in the way. True, there are many challenging things that we will experience in life, and we know that the only certainty is change, so we will always face upheavals. This doesn't mean that *all* of life is bad; it just means that life is not easy. But happiness does not come from your circumstances or your situation. Happiness comes from a choice that you make within.

Learning how to choose happiness

I've had to train my brain to choose happiness, even when my circumstances suggested the opposite. I believe I've boosted my natural happiness set point by carrying out specific 'feel happier' activities. If you're struggling to find the root of happiness, incorporate these personal tips into your daily life, and you may start to feel happier. Stick at it, put in the hard work, and you should see results.

1. Choose gratitude and look on the bright side

No matter how bad life seems, there's always something positive you can find to focus on. It could be the fact you have a place to live, friends and family that love you, have clothes to wear, or even that you have eyes to see and legs to walk with. There are millions of people in the world that don't have some of these things.

Since happiness is a choice, start finding things in your life that you're grateful for. It could also be seemingly small, general things that we often take for granted, such as the smell of cut grass, the sound of the ocean, etc. Writing these things down in a gratitude journal helps to solidify your happiness further.

2. Choose to think positively

Try to live by the 'every cloud has a silver lining' anecdote. Focusing on positive thoughts and trying to reduce negative thinking is easier said than done but give the following technique a try. Each time you have a negative thought, simply replace it with a positive one. This practice will help to retrain your habitual thought patterns to bring more positive thoughts and happiness into your life.

Changing your perspective on your situation will help you find happiness. If you've made a mistake – however big – try to focus on your past achievements instead, actually visualizing your previous successes and happy times.

3. Choose to smile

Turn that frown upside down! Smiling and other external expressions work as a continual feedback loop, helping to reinforce our internal emotions. So, smiling even when we feel down will gradually make us feel happier (and healthier). Try smiling at strangers, too: as well as being a choice; happiness is also contagious.

4. Choose to be more mindful

Mindfulness meditation is an easy way to try to increase your happiness levels. Start your day with just 10-15 minutes of meditation shortly after waking: the immediate heightened inner clarity and focus it will give you will set you up for what's ahead.

Many studies have shown that meditation can boost happiness levels by reducing stress hormones, shrinking the part of the brain that controls anxiety, and stopping rumination, amongst other things. No matter how bad life seems, there's always something positive you can find to focus on. Since happiness is a choice, start finding things in your life that you're grateful for.

5. Choose a purpose

Meaningfulness is a happy factor that you can extend into your whole life. Whether it's volunteering, gardening, or becoming politically active, activities with a purpose have been shown to boost people's happiness and reduce stress levels at the same time.

6. Choose to be satisfied

"Comparison is the thief of joy." We've all heard it before. And in today's Insta-ready society, this rings true more than ever. In a social media savvy world, flaunting your money, travels, and other supposed successes or happiness is all too common, especially with the younger generation. However, if happiness is a choice, then comparing yourself to other people will only result in unhappiness.

Choose to be satisfied with what you have and stop comparing your life to that of others: reduce the time you spend scrolling through social media.

Now, after all of that, if you still aren't happy:

Be blessed.

4

A STRANGER WILL SUPPORT YOU BEFORE ANYONE ELSE & YOU BETTER NOT CRY ABOUT IT!

BE BLESSED: *REFLECTIONS OF INTROSPECT*

It is what it is. That's it, that's all. I wouldn't leave you hanging like that without any explanation, but that's really how I feel. That's it, and that's all.

Support is needed to thrive in any area of life. We exude intrinsic motivation, but support gives us the push and courage to keep going and let's not forget the dollars. But what happens when you realize that a great deal of your support is not family, friends or close relatives one day? Do you give up, quit, and worry yourself about what you could have done differently? Girl bye. I have my own reasons as to why I believe strangers support you before anyone else, and because this is my book, I guess that's the only opinion that matters at this point. So here we go.

The people closest to us sometimes get defensive because they are trying to protect us, but they could also be trying to protect themselves. Your personal growth or business aspirations could be intimidating to them, a reminder of their own lack of action.

When we begin to step into our power, we surprise people around us, especially those who know us to be a "certain way." When we start making some noise, and our confidence pushes us to take risks, this can alarm our family and friends, who may not know how to react to the "new" you. Some may even feel that by supporting you in your journey to success that you will "change" and forget about them in the process. Clearly, this has nothing to do with you and everything to do with the person who feels intimidated. *Don't allow the lack of support from your family and friends to deter you from following your bliss.* Maybe they'll come around and warm up to the new "you," maybe they won't.

People you meet, strangers who become acquaintances and acquaintances who turn into friends are likely to have less judgement over you - they don't know your past, they only get what they see, and for some, who you are today does not threaten them in any way.

We are expressing a side of ourselves they wish they could, but for some reason, feel they can't. Some people just don't realize how uncomfortable it is for us to "live out our dreams" and stand out from the crowd. They don't see the day-to-day struggle of stepping outside of our comfort zone to make a difference in this world because all they see is this effortless, "pretty perfect world" that we are living in, which is not precise at all. Anyone chasing their dreams can feel excited, powerful and confident all at the same time while being scared as hell, frustrated and alone.

If only they knew what it was really like for us, maybe then they would realize that we are just trying to live our lives to the fullest, looking to feel supported.

The reality is, when someone feels like they can't have something you have, it is normal for them to be distant towards you, **only because what you have is a reminder of what they don't have** - *be it self-confidence, a thriving business, a newfound love.*

Have you ever noticed how quickly you could build rapport with someone you meet for the first time who shares the same interests as you, and you simply *"click"?* You *"click"* for a reason, and the reason is that they have caught the "vibe" you are putting out there. **Those who catch onto "your vibe" are likely to be similar to you, and when you are exuding confidence, they can't help but catch the "vibe" that exists**

within themselves. This is where the MAGIC happens!

They simply don't get it. I mean, how can you take such a big risk, be so vulnerable, open, bold, and so courageous?? Don't you want to play it safe? Some people in our lives are comfortable where they are in their own lives; they are happy with who they surround themselves with and content with the life they have created for themselves. **Someone who "dares to be different," who wants MORE out of life and reaches for it, however, is often misunderstood by people who are complacent in life.**

It is exhausting and energy-consuming to convince people of your perspective and where you're coming from. Instead, wish them well and keep doing YOU! The world awaits your brilliance; so, there you have it! I've had this conversation with too many people struggling with trying to "convince" their family and friends to support them that I had to write about it. The minute I put myself in their shoes and tried to understand an unsupportive family member or friend's perspective - was the day I realized that it had nothing to do with me at all.

5

GIVE YOURSELF PERMISSION TO DO WHAT'S RIGHT FOR YOU

Imagine that you're getting ready to start your day.

You have your coffee mug in your hand. You peek out the window to see what the weather looks like, and then you head to your closet to get dressed.

But you don't stress out about which outfit to wear, because your clothes are just clothes, not armor to protect you from other people's opinions.

And later, when you see other people, you don't wonder what the right thing to say is because your belonging does not depend on whether they agree with the words that come out of your mouth.

You don't worry about being too much or too loud or too quiet or too anything.

You don't waste your time trying to fit in because you are in the business of creating belonging.

Instead, you bring your whole self wherever you go because that is how you move through the world: confident, grounded, comfortable in your own skin, with an understanding of who you are and what you're about.

That's what we all want, right?

We all want belonging, connection, and confidence, and to feel comfortable in our own skin and to believe we're okay as we are.

But the problem is, we've been taught to chase the shadows of those things instead of the real deal.

So, we work on trying to look like we've got it all together instead of connecting over the fact that we don't. We try to fake it till we make it instead of growing our confidence right where we are.

We spend our time and energy trying to fit in, and pretending to be okay when we're not, and keeping busy—instead of resting in the truth that we are already enough.

But all those things we're doing—the pretending, the hiding behind cute earrings and a fake smile, the surface-level conversations—all those things that feel safe are actually moving us FARTHER AWAY from where we want to be.

The solution is to give yourself permission to be who you really are.

It took me a long time to figure this out.

See, I always understood all the Life Rules I was supposed to follow, but I could never actually follow them all.

I couldn't follow the rules about looking just right and not being too weird, or the rules about not taking up space, or the rules about buying all the right things.

I had way too many feelings to follow the rules about being low-maintenance or quiet or go-with-the-flow. I had too many opinions to be "nice" all the time.

I just could not be the person the world seemed to expect me to be.

I did try. I did! And when that didn't work, I tried to pretend at least that I had it all together.

But pretending to have it all together kept me apart from everyone else because I couldn't let them see the real me.

It took me a long time to discover the truth. The truth is, I don't have to hide my true self. The truth is, I am not broken, and neither are you.

The truth is, I am the way I am for a damn good reason.

The truth is, I am allowed to give myself permission to be who I really am.

When you give yourself permission to be who you really are, you start to get comfortable in your own skin. You start to trust yourself because you learn to listen to yourself.

The people in your life can see you for who you really are. You don't have any more questions about whether your people would still love you IF THEY KNEW because THEY KNEW. They know what you're really like because you show them, and you tell them. Being seen and known is the beginning of belonging.

The other thing that happens is this: you question yourself less because you know yourself more.

You don't chase everything everyone else says you should. You don't say yes when you mean no. You don't hide what you want. Whatever that thing is in your heart that you want to chase, you do that because that is what you're here to do.

Other people can have their opinions. You get to have yourself and your dreams and your LIFE.

That's what happens when you give yourself permission to be who you really are. You get your life back. This is the permission slip you need to stop trying to live someone else's version of your life and step into the truth of who you are.

6

MAKE A DIFFERENCE IN THE WORLD BY SIMPLY LIVING IN IT

DR. CRYSHAUNDA RORIE

Are you living, or are you simply existing? You're living? Great! Congrats. We can move right along.

7

LEAVE HIM WHERE YOU MET HIM. SOMETIMES

I guess that's why I rushed through number seven because this one gets a little juicy. Where did you meet yours at? Mine was at a church, and honeyyyyyy, I should have let God deliver him & me before those lines were crossed, but anyway, this is about us, not them, so let's continue down this loophole.

The fact of the matter is, we hear all the time "watch for the red flags," then we sit there like the three blind mice and somehow become immune to seeing what reality really is. We've all been dumb for someone or something and have really downplayed our self-worth to feel "loved". But time out for all of that! Playtime is over.

Our hearts should not be childish because we continuously downplay what our ears hear, our eyes see, and our minds think. Most of us will have at least one, if not a few, significant relationships during our lifetime. Our first intimate encounters may be more difficult or challenging because we're new to the experience of forming an intimate bond with another person and may not really know what we're doing and what to expect. But time and experience should help us navigate through future relationships in a much better way.

It's essential to get to know yourself in every possible way before you move into a committed relationship. Often, individuals go in search of a relationship without this essential knowledge. But how can you ever hope to know another individual if you don't know yourself first? How can you address another's needs and desires if you're disconnected from your own?

As obvious as these issues may appear, and as much as you may feel you understand them intellectually, it should come as no surprise that what initially seems unimportant may take on greater significance as insights occur over the course of the relationship. In retrospect, individuals are often baffled about their own behavior and expectations in a relationship.

A really good exercise I ask my clients to do is to write down every partner they've had a significant relationship with, and then, for each, answer questions such as: What attracted you to this person initially? Did the attraction last? Was your fantasy about this person—what you imagined or assumed to be true—validated in reality? How long did the relationship last? Did revelations during the course of the relationship change your mind? What was the deal-breaker? Do any patterns — i.e., similarities from that relationship to other relationships — emerge?

Learn to ask the hard questions out of the gate the first or second time you meet someone before opinions are solidly formed. Most of us seem to do much better when we have no real expectations of someone because we hardly know who they are and are not yet trying to impress them.

And watch for red flags—indicators that something needs to be questioned or otherwise validated. Often these are clues that something may be trouble in the future. Here are my few red flags that no one could get past without a doubt.

1. Lack of communication.

These individuals find it difficult to talk about issues or express how they feel. Often, when it would seem most important to be open and honest, they distance themselves emotionally, leaving their partner hanging or having to deal with a situation on their own. Whatever is "communicated" is often expressed through moodiness and sometimes the dreaded "silent treatment."

2. Irresponsible, immature, and unpredictable.

Some people have trouble mastering basic life skills—taking care of themselves, managing their finances and personal space, holding onto a job, and making plans for their life and future. Small crises surrounding how they live their daily lives may take up a lot of time and energy. If so, there may be little time and energy left for you and your issues. These people may still be working on growing up. In other words, it may be hard to rely on them for almost anything.

3. Lack of trust.

When a person has difficulty being honest with himself or herself, it may be hard for them to be honest with you. Some of this behavior may not be calculated and malicious but simply a learned way or habit of coping. However, being out-and-out lied to is a no-brainer. A person who holds himself or herself unaccountable for their actions lacks integrity and lacks respect for their partner. You may feel, and rightly so, that there are a lot of "missing pieces," so much that you don't know or that is purposely hidden from you.

4. Feeling insecure in the relationship.

You may often feel that you don't know where you stand in a relationship. Rather than moving forward, building on shared experiences that should be strengthening your connection, you feel uncomfortable, uncertain, or anxious about where it's heading. You may seek reassurances from your partner, but somehow these are only momentary and fleeting. As a result, you may be working double duty to keep the relationship on track while your partner contributes little.

5. The relationship is built on the need to feel needed.

Often, we enter into a relationship strongly identified with our needs. The need may be that you, my partner, must do certain things for me to make me feel secure and satisfied, or that you allow me, your partner, to feel needed by fulfilling your needs. However, if this dynamic is the focal point of a relationship, there may be little room for real growth, individually or as a couple.

Now, if they have passed these, they may just be the one or maybe just another lesson of life. No matter what, go with your gut! Stand up for your heart and take charge of your life. It matters.

8
YOU'RE ENOUGH

And if someone ever tells you that you aren't, dismiss them respectfully. I believe that you are enough, just as you are, just as you were made to be. But I want to be clear about what that means and what it does not mean.

Because "you are enough" does not mean that you have been measured and considered and judged and that you have finally earned the label of "enough."

It doesn't mean that you've worked long enough, tried hard enough, presented well enough. It's simply who you are. The you that you are is enough.

You don't have to be more, or do more, or buy more to be who you are meant to be.

That's what I mean when I say you are enough.

You are enough does not mean that you are a final product, complete and finished, all done growing and changing and learning things forevermore.

That you are enough does not mean that you are all-powerful and perfect, either. That you are

enough does not mean that you are everything.

The pursuit of enough flies in the face of the pursuit of everything. Having a good grasp on "enough" means you don't have to get everything, and you certainly don't have to be everything.

You are enough does not mean that you have to be self-sufficient. It doesn't mean that you don't need anyone or anything else. It means you understand how much you do need, how small you are in this great grand universe — and that you don't have to be even one inch bigger than that.

That you are absolutely enough does not mean that you'll never need help. When you know you are enough, it's easier to ask for help. It's easier to admit your weaknesses. You know that your imperfections and your difficulties don't reflect on your worth because you are already enough, just as you are.

You are enough does not mean that you are flawless or that you never make mistakes.

You know that you make mistakes. You

know that I make mistakes. I make mistakes every single day. I am aware of my flaws before I even roll out of bed every day.

That doesn't mean that my flaws are the truest, most important thing about me; it just means that I acknowledge them. I see them there. They exist. (Hi, flaws! YOU'RE MINE.)

If "being enough" means "being perfect," then you are enough is just another reason to hide your true self. You hear that kind of "you are enough," and you think: well! I know I'm not perfect, so either I'm not enough, or I have to hide who I really am.

No.

You are enough means that you were made to be you, as you are, on purpose.
It is no mistake that you are this person, in this place, at this time.

You are enough as you are, mess and all, beautiful and broken, showing up for your life every day. That's all you have to be and all you have to do. You're already enough.

You are enough means you can grow and change and continue to become because you aren't trying to prove yourself. You're just trying to be yourself.

You are enough means that you don't have to strive to become more worthy, valid, acceptable, or loved. You already are all of those things.

There are things you might want to be more of. More open. More honest. More true. More authentic. Freer. More connected. More intentional. More purposeful. Those are all expressions of your enough-ness. They aren't about changing yourself; they're about being yourself.

You were enough before, you are enough now, and you will continue to be enough as you become more of who you were made to be. And believing that, when the world keeps whispering otherwise, is brave.

That's what I mean when I say that you are enough.

And you are.

9

ONLY CONSUME WHAT NOURISHES

BE BLESSED: *REFLECTIONS OF INTROSPECT*

What nourishes you behind the plate? Have you ever thought about that? When most people think of nourishment, it's usually in the form of a healthy diet – plenty of fruits, vegetables, whole grains, proteins, and water. But while wholesome food is certainly essential for physical growth, is it enough to satisfy your hunger for life? True health means more than just the body's physical condition, and the food we eat is often secondary to the experiences and excitement in our lives. This energy fulfills us on a multi-dimensional level that includes the physical, mental, emotional, and spiritual. If one of these areas is out of balance, it could drain your ability to create an overall vibrant state of health and happiness.

Assessing your relationships, physical activity, career, and spirituality, can help pinpoint where you are feeling unsatisfied and why. More importantly, figuring out what you need to do in order to regain balance can provide the motivation you need to make changes. This will not only nourish the parts of you that may be starving for attention but foster the personal environment necessary to thrive in all aspects of life. Here are five ways to feed your spirit:

1. Do what you love.

Wouldn't it be nice to have a career that is aligned with your passion in life? Even if you have a busy day, your perception of stress would be far lower in a job where you're working towards something you believe in. Less stress means better health, a happier mood, and a more positive influence on others.

If you're currently unhappy in your job, don't settle for just being content and comfortable because the pay is decent. Do a little soul-searching and ask yourself what you would do every day if there were no limitations. Pursue that vision with your whole heart!

2. Surround yourself with supportive people.

Your level of happiness is directly dependent upon the moods of those around you, so why let yourself be dragged down by negative people who constantly deflate you? Gravitate instead towards those who encourage you to strive towards fulfilling your goals and share in the joy of your accomplishments. It will propel you to new heights.

3. Listen to your body.

Everybody is unique. People widely vary in which foods make them feel great or awful, how far they can push their endurance, how sensitive they are to the stimuli around them, and what they need to feel their best. If your intuition tells you that something doesn't feel right, avoid it—no matter how many others tell you it has been beneficial for them. Only you know what is best for you, so make a habit of observing your body's subtle signals.

4. Connect with something bigger than yourself.

It can be easy to get caught up in the tangles of daily living and lose sight of what really matters in life, such as health, happiness, and love. Whether it's practicing meditation or visiting a church, making time for spiritual practice will go a long way in keeping you grounded, peaceful, and clear in your vision of the future.

5. Learn and grow.

One of the biggest benefits of living in the modern age of unlimited access to information is that there are always new opportunities to expand your knowledge. Whether it's acquiring new skills to further your career, boosting your creative abilities, or taking a personal development course, learning new things can contribute to your zest for life while keeping the door open to new possibilities.

How do you plan to nourish your spirit?

10

THE DEVIL DOESN'T CARE

Point. Blank. Period.
He doesn't care.

We aren't going to stay on this subject too long because we don't want the big bad devil to think we are giving him any type of clout. Boy, sit down! It's no secret that competency is always relative. Everyone has their own strengths and weaknesses, and that's how God meant it to be. Yet somehow, the enemy still uses our incompetency to attack our identity and security, and sometimes his schemes work.

2 Corinthians 12: 9 KJV tells us, "But he said to me, 'My grace is sufficient for you, for my power is made perfect in weakness.' Therefore, I will boast all the more gladly of my weaknesses, so that Christ's power may rest on me."

Weakness was never meant to be the enemy's weapon to cause sin and confusion but to be God's tool to build faith and reliance on Him.

Here are four ways that the enemy will try to use your weakness against you and how to counter by standing on God's original design.

Fear Over Faith

Where there is a limitation, Satan will often try to lure us into fear when facing uncertainty. Many times, when the early disciples would allow fear to take the better of them, Jesus would correct them lovingly by pointing out their "little faith."

Weaknesses in the light of God's love will cause us to trust and rely fully on God, not doubt Him. 1 John 4:18 KJV declares to us, "There is no fear in love, but perfect love casts out fear. For fear has to do with punishment, and whoever fears has not been perfected in love."

Failure Over Freedom

Weakness will very often lead to a mistake or even a failure. In my personal life, I have always seen my inabilities to cause mishaps at work or even in my family. But amid failure, I am assured that God can and will turn situations around.

But sometimes, we are tricked into thinking that God cannot conquer our failures. This causes us to live in bondage instead of freedom. Proverbs 4:16 KJV tells us, "For the righteous falls seven times and rises again, but the wicked stumble in times of calamity."

Regret Over Redemption

One of the enemy's favorite toys is our regret. He plays with it and wants us to do the same. But God has one desire for our regrets: He wants them laid at the foot of the cross because Christ paid the price for your redemption from any past mistake or failure.

The blood of Christ has already redeemed you from any sin or weakness. God's power is made evident in our inabilities. We can now walk free and sanctified not by our own strengths but by God's infinite strength.

Works Over Will

When we fail, and it's clear that there's no conceivable way to make things right on our own, God intervenes. But sometimes, the devil whispers into our ears that God is too far away or too busy to help us out.

But God promises in Deuteronomy 31:6 KJV, "Be strong and courageous. Do not fear or be in dread of them, for it is the LORD your God who goes with you. He will not leave you or forsake you."

Our courage and confidence lie in God's pleasing and perfect will, not our good works. We can trust God even in the midst of our weakness because He is working for our good. So always remember that the devil doesn't care, but our God does.

11

UNAPOLOGETICALLY DOPE

BE BLESSED: *REFLECTIONS OF INTROSPECT*

Being "Unapologetically Dope" is a continuous process. It means making a decision each day to be the best version of yourself, no matter what! Unapologetically means without "regret," and dope means the "best!" Combining and embodying these words, you'll find that you can become a better version of yourself without regret about your past life experiences without holding anything back!

For me, being unapologetically dope starts with my willingness to be an authentic and transparent version of myself. Transparency includes my willingness to share my story and help others I come in contact with, giving them everything I have acquired mentally, not from only education but from experience, downfalls, what I've tried, what I've implemented and what I know works.

How dope are you? Are you dope enough to be honest, transparent and real? Yes, it can be tough, confusing, and nerve-wracking to open up, but think about those you can help and will help by sharing a few words, a testimony, an experience, and a true encounter. Are we clear?

12

YOUR MOUTH IS YOUR WEAKNESS, SIS

DR. CRYSHAUNDA RORIE

Be quiet! Shut up! Zip it! Whewwww! Letting your mouth hinder your growth and opportunity is not acceptable. Sometimes your mouth can be your worst enemy, whether you want to agree or not. Your words, your dreams, and your thoughts have the power to create conditions in your life. What you speak about, you can bring about. God spoke the world into existence; you were created in His image. So be mindful that you are a speaking Spirit.

If you keep saying you can't stand your job, you might lose your job.

If you keep saying you can't stand your body, your body can become sick.

If you keep saying you can't stand your car, your car could be stolen or just stop operating.

If you keep saying you're broke, guess what? You'll always be broke.

If you keep saying you can't trust a man or trust a woman, you will always find someone in your life to hurt and betray you.

If you keep saying you can't find a job, you will

remain unemployed.

If you keep saying you can't find someone to love you or believe in you, your very thought will attract more experiences to confirm your beliefs.

If you keep talking about a divorce or break up in a relationship, then you might end up with it.

Turn your thoughts and conversations around to be more positive and power packed with faith, hope, love and action.

Don't be afraid to believe that you can have what you say you want and deserve.

Watch your Thoughts; they become words.

Watch your Words; they become actions.

Watch your Actions; they become habits.

Watch your Habits, for they become your character.

Watch your Character, for it becomes your Destiny.

BE BLESSED: *REFLECTIONS OF INTROSPECT*

Repeat this daily!!

In the search for Me, I discovered Truth.

In the search for Truth, I discovered Love.

In the search for Love, I discovered GOD.

And in God, I have found Everything.

Be Blessed

13
EVERYTHING YOU NEED IS IN YOU

We fail to see that what we seek outside us is already within us. We can give ourselves validation, satisfaction, permission and love. Paradoxically, when we give these things to ourselves, we are much more likely to get them from other people.

PERMISSION

Around the world, people are waiting for permission. Artists, authors, musicians, and actors are waiting to be picked by the gallery owner, publisher, record label, and movie producer. But we live in a world where it's possible to give yourself permission. There's never been a greater time in history for people who are creative. We have almost free access to tools, resources, and distribution channels.

- Authors can publish their books on Amazon without permission from a publisher.
- Musicians can upload their tracks to iTunes without permission from a record label.

- Filmmakers can distribute their movies on Amazon Prime without permission from a studio.

The gates have fallen, and the so-called gatekeepers aren't sitting around waiting to reject your book, your album, or your startup. Their livelihood depends on saying yes.

- Editors need to find good books to publish.
- Record labels need great musicians.
- Venture capitalists need a great startup to invest in.

But if you aren't willing to start until they give you permission, you've shot yourself in the foot. Like almost everything else, if you give yourself permission, you paradoxically start to get it from other people. I gave myself permission to write a book and publish it. It was the most valuable thing I've done for my career. As a result, I received permission from a publisher.

VALIDATION

We seek it from our parents, peers, mentors, teachers and strangers on the internet. But the last place we usually look for validation is within. Yet, the professional self-validates.

In Indian culture, most kids are raised with very high expectations from their parents, and as a result, kids seek their validation. I spent years seeking validation from my mom. Even though she was proud, it would never be expressed according to my expectations.

It got to the point that everything that I was seeking from my mom, I had to give to myself. This is easier said than done because we all have a deep need to be validated. But it's only letting go of that when we become the most fully self-expressed, no-bullshit versions of ourselves.

LOVE

Love has nothing to do with someone else. It is all about you. It is a way of being. It essentially means you have brought sweetness into your emotion... Even if a loved one is not physically with you anymore, you are still capable of loving. So, what is love then? It is your own quality. You are only using the other person as a key to open up what is already within you.

We don't look for anything outside of ourselves as much as we do for love. We look for it from our parents, friends, and romantic partners. All of the things mentioned above are really a search for reassurance that we're loved.

As someone whose primary love languages are physical touch and words of affirmation, I've always wanted love to be expressed in that way. I want to date men who can't keep their hands off of me and whose words are like music to my ears. But I've also grown up in a culture where public displays of affection are uncommon, and love isn't expressed verbally.

We all want to be seen, heard and above all things, loved. But we also have an expectation of what that looks like, how that love is expressed from parents, peers, friends, and romantic partners. With that expectation, we attempt to fill an internal void with external validation. But this kind of love leaks; it doesn't fill us up. We have holes in our hearts because we don't love ourselves. But if we choose to give love to ourselves, we can be kinder to ourselves. When we screw up, we can be gentler with ourselves when we fail.

When we expect love to be expressed in a certain way and it's not, we overlook what love is. The love in my family isn't expressed according to my love languages. But it's something that can certainly be felt in the meals we eat, moments we share, and conversations we have. Here are some thought-provoking questions that you should consider with love.

- Do you believe that you are worthy of your own time, your own love and your own money?
- Do you ever dress up for no reason? Just for you?
- Do you treat yourself with love, care, and respect?
- Do you treat yourself as well as you treat other people?

Notice how NONE of those questions is about how we get love from others, but how we give it to ourselves. We can't expect other people to fill our hearts or make us feel whole and complete. It doesn't matter if it's permission, validation, or love. When we expect to get those things from other people, that not only puts unrealistic pressure on them, but we enter situations in our lives from a place of scarcity and deficiency.

When we assume our hearts can only be filled with love from outside of us, we go through the world feeling deficient in some way. Searching outside of yourself for everything that's already within you allows you to avoid responsibility. Realize that everything you're searching for outside of you is already within you. Then, you'll have agency over your life in a way that you never had before.

14

GET OUT OF
YOUR OWN WAY

Getting out of the way means becoming very familiar with your inner world. You discover what you do that makes you suffer, so you can choose peace instead.

Amazingly, you realize that you can press pause at any moment and step back from the momentum of old, recycled habits.

When you do, you see what is actually happening: the pain of being stuck in an old resentment that has been dragging you down, the constricting effect of believing your thoughts, and the chaos that comes from letting your feelings rule.

With your eyes wide open, you are primed to live in ways that are intelligent, affirming, and aligned with your deepest desires. Finally, clarity arrives.

Getting out of the way looks like this:

DR. CRYSHAUNDA RORIE

Ask yourself, "In this moment, what do I really want to feel?"

The answer connects you with your true intention to **be happy**, peaceful, and clear. Already, you are halfway to being free.

Notice the thoughts and feelings that grab your attention.

See how you get in the way of happiness. Do you live in a belief that you are inadequate? Do you tell yourself you are a victim of your past? Do you define yourself by sadness or fear? This is why you suffer.

Befriend your experience by noting what is present but know that it doesn't have to control you.

Just for now, don't hold onto your stressful stories. Let your feelings be without acting on them. This is the most loving way you can be with yourself.

Experience the space that remains when thoughts and feelings no longer hook you.

Even if only for a moment, you've discovered what it's like to get out of the way.

BE BLESSED: *REFLECTIONS OF INTROSPECT*

Here you are—whole and relaxed, ripe to enjoy yourself, to make wise decisions that come from love, not fear and limitation. You see that life can be so beautifully simple. You touch into the living possibility of happiness for you.

There is **no need to change your thoughts** or get rid of any emotions to get out of the way. Just become aware of your inner experience. Realize how defining you by it constrains you.

Notice that you can make a choice to live fully now, beyond any self-imposed boundaries, with a clear mind and open heart.

It is the effortless, practical way to happiness available in each moment.

Finally Fully Living

When you get out of the way, you stop resisting life. The focus shifts from what you don't have to what is here and available. No longer doubting everything, you receive what life offers you.

And rather than living in the mind-created past or future, you are available to the simplicity of this now moment.

Unclouded by mental noise, you become crystal clear about what to do next. You tell the truth about what is and isn't working. And you take practical steps to begin truly living.

As I became aware of habits that were hijacking my happiness, I discovered why my relationships weren't lasting and began making different choices. I realized how fear had been keeping me from living fully. I began seeing everything through the eyes of love.

Really, it's true. When you get out of the way, your life will shine…endlessly.

15

END OF STORY

Well, well, well, we have come to the end. I hope you enjoyed my reflections of introspection. In my 32 years of living, I have encountered the best, the worst, the iffy and the courage to do things like this; spill my guts. No literally.

Please share this work with your friends, colleagues, family members and your ex. They more than likely could benefit from it. Continue to grow and mold yourself to be the best version of yourself. The world needs your gifts, your inspiration and especially your testimony. Thank you for sowing into my life by taking part in this journey.

As always, Be Blessed.

ABOUT THE AUTHOR

Dr. Cryshaunda Rorie is an ambitious woman who thrives on making a difference in the lives of those in her local community by empowering, leading, fostering, nurturing, and strengthening beyond borders. She is the founder of Queens Appreciate Queens, a women's group that meets monthly to do volunteer work around High Point, NC. Cryshaunda is also the founder of I Am Blair's Closet LLC, a children's clothing boutique named after her five-year-old daughter Blair Noelle and Suited by Cryshaunda, an online boutique for working women's wear.

Cryshaunda is a thrice published author. Her most recent book, *Be Blessed: Reflections of Introspect* is a thought-provoking work that provokes inner evaluation and self-motivation. She is the author of *Confessions from Cancer: Know Your Role*, a book that journeys through the life of Cryshaunda's personal cancer survivor story, and *A Trip To Blair's Closet*, a book that focuses on self-awareness and self-esteem in young ladies.

Born and raised in High Point, NC, Cryshaunda has been actively transforming the beliefs of those who give up on inner-city youth by using her personal upbringing as a platform for success. She uses personal experience, both positive and negative, to encourage and motivate those she comes in contact with. Cryshaunda believes that with the power she possesses, it is her duty to show another light, a positive light, for all genders, races & backgrounds in her community.

ABOUT THE AUTHOR

Dr. Cryshaunda Rorie is an ambitious woman who thrives on making a difference in the lives of those in her local community by empowering, leading, fostering, nurturing, and strengthening beyond borders. She is the founder of Queens Appreciate Queens, a women's group that meets monthly to do volunteer work around High Point, NC. Cryshaunda is also the founder of I Am Blair's Closet LLC, a children's clothing boutique named after her five-year-old daughter Blair Noelle and Suited by Cryshaunda, an online boutique for working women's wear.

Cryshaunda is a thrice published author. Her most recent book, *Be Blessed: Reflections of Introspect* is a thought-provoking work that provokes inner evaluation and self-motivation. She is the author of *Confessions from Cancer: Know Your Role*, a book that journeys through the life of Cryshaunda's personal cancer survivor story, and *A Trip To Blair's Closet*, a book that focuses on self-awareness and self-esteem in young ladies.

Born and raised in High Point, NC, Cryshaunda has been actively transforming the beliefs of those who give up on inner-city youth by using her personal upbringing as a platform for success. She uses personal experience, both positive and negative, to encourage and motivate those she comes in contact with. Cryshaunda believes that with the power she possesses, it is her duty to show another light, a positive light, for all genders, races & backgrounds in her community.

www.ingramcontent.com/pod-product-compliance
Lightning Source LLC
Chambersburg PA
CBHW050651160426
43194CB00010B/1902